First published in the United States of America in 2006 by
Universe Publishing
A Division of Rizzoli International Publications, Inc.
300 Park Avenue South
New York, NY 10010
ww.rizzoliusa.com

Originally published in 2005 by Edizioni Gribaudo

ISBN 0-7893-1392-8
Library of Congress Control Number 2005907166

2006 2007 2008 2009 / 10 9 8 7 6 5 4 3 2 1

Printed in Italy

Editor
Nacho Asensio

Editorial Coordination
Joaquim Ballarín i Bargalló

Documentation
Mariona Villavieja i García
Joaquim Ballarín i Bargalló

Texts
Maria Cinta Martí i Amela
Joaquim Ballarín i Bargalló

Graphic Design
Argüelles Gutiérrez Disseny

Layout
Anna Soler i Feliu

Translation
Mark Parent
Maurizio Siliato
Zita Morais

Contents

Introduction

Wood, which has been used for building since the dawn of man, is blessed with a variety of characteristics that afford it great versatility. Used for structural work, it is also effective for insulating against temperature and noise and is very environmentally friendly. Its uses in interior decorating are practically unlimited, not to mention some of its more subjective traits such as warmth, texture, and touch.

Current thinking has it that wood as a raw material is a renewable natural resource of unlimited supply. Pressure from the ecology sectors has led to ever more computerized and automated systems of cutting and transforming wood. This in turn has afforded countless products that are made from wood by-products thus optimizing the use of this natural resource. Important advances have also been made in cementing and joining wood, in wood renovation, and in antipest products, which grant long-term protection and conserve the wood.

Thanks to these advances wood is a key element in prefabrication construction. Here, the majority of the elaboration is done in the factory or workshop, thus saving time and allowing ultramodern machinery to be used. This provides us with a light, totally recyclable product that can be easily transported and whose installation does not require specialized labor.

Log Cabin

This is the oldest of wood constructions whose origin would seem to be from Northern Europe. With the waves of migration its use became extended as long as quality wood could be found in abundance. Initially, construction consisted of placing round trunks, without the bark, horizontally one atop the other and joining them at the ends or the corners. Later, with the appearance of sawmills, the size of the logs became uniform and standardized.

Nowadays, this type of building system is commercialized in kits that contain totally prefabricated parts that can be quickly and easily set up at the site. Presently a vast array of finishes, such as smooth, rough hewn, stained, antique look, and painted, are sold. Likewise, diverse shapes are available that are a far cry from the simple, square original ones.

Heavy Framework

In this system of building there is a well-braced structure of large, heavy pillars and girders in modulelike sections. This supports another secondary structure of smaller girders. It appeared in Europe and China in Neolithic times and later spread to North America, Japan, and Southeast Asia. It was most widely used between the end of the Middle Ages and the nineteenth century. Its modern version appeared in Europe at the end of the 1960s and in Japan in the 1980s. It brought with it new fastening and joining systems that use steel, which afford more strength and facilitate prefabrication and automatization.

Light Framework

The heavy framework evolved towards this new system in the United States in the nineteenth century. It does not require specific materials for the load-bearing structures and the enclosing and roof elements, but rather the same panels and walls serve the two functions. The panels are put together with nails or staples. This modulelike system affords high standardization, great flexibility, and ideally lends itself to prefabrication. Wood panels, which came on the scene in the second half of the twentieth century, proved to be a revolution in regards to the structural framework. The most emblematic of these is the plywood panel whose evolution is closely tied to the development of adhesives.

Laminated Wood

Laminated wood using glue made its appearance at the beginning of the twentieth century where it was utilized for manufacturing straight beams of great length. Curved beams would appear later on. It is based on techniques similar to light framework; it uses small cross-sections to build elements of almost unlimited dimensions. Beginning with the International Exposition in Brussels in 1910, it enjoyed widespread acceptance especially in Central Europe and Switzerland. After 1923, it began to be used outside of Europe. By the end of the 1930s, its quality was well acclaimed. Due to the restrictions on steel imposed by the Second World War, its use became firmly and definitively established. At the same time, the invention of synthetic adhesives permitted laminated wood to be employed practically anywhere, without the previous restrictions on indoor use.

01

Wood
in the Landscape

Wood is an element that integrates to a high degree and its role in integrating into the landscape is very important. The projects in this chapter become the absolute masters of their environment as they establish a dialogue with it; in this dialogue between equals, they create their own private space or they become an integral, almost necessary, part of the landscape.

Maison Convercey
Capture the Landscape

BERNAT QUIROT AND OLIVIER VICHARD/
QUIROT - VICHARD ARCHITECTES
COLLABORATORS: Alexandre LENOBLE,
Emmanuel BEAUDOIN
PHOTO: ©Luc Boegly

GRACHAUX – FRANCE – 2001

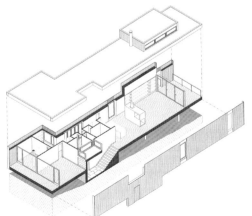

Elevated above the terrain by way of pillars, the building lightly flows over the unbroken countryside. From the inside, it is masterly designed to offer perfect views of the picture-framed exterior. The building, narrow and extending out to each end, takes on the appearance of a kaleidoscope through which we are afforded a vast array of views of the unfolding landscape around it.

A light steel structure, assembled in only two weeks, is delightfully clad with wood that perfectly integrates what would seem to be a rather stern volume into its setting. The access to the door is the only contact with the terrain and it acts as a point of balance and connection for this tetrahedron that is floating on a sea of green.

Slight variations in height for the different rooms, shrewdly calculated apertures, and the nonstop dialogue between the interior and exterior enrich the design that purposely subdues its impact on the setting. Inside, the spatial flow is only interrupted in order to delimit the dining and living room spaces.

Maison Goulet

Warm Refuge

SAÏA BARBARESE TOPOUZANOV ARCHITECTES
PHOTO: ©Marc Cramer, Frédéric Saia

SANTE MARGUERITE DU LAC MASSON– CANADA – 2003

Isolated in a rough and rugged setting, the outline of this dwelling brings to mind the image of a refuge. Placed on terrain that slopes down from north to south to the shores of a lake, the construction is placed on a flat, rocky plot that extends out from east to west. Two large stone chimneys seem to anchor the wooden structure to the terrain. A zinc covering gives it a velvetlike texture, almost cold, which contrasts with the warmth that emanates from the interior.

When the weather permits, the large doors and glass walls are opened, thus dissolving the walls and allowing the exterior spaces to prolong the interior ones. On the second floor, the windows on both sides are in harmony as they afford views of the surrounding terrain and the slope below.

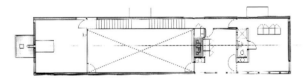

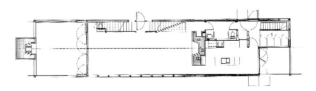

As architecture that is deeply rooted in and conditioned by the climate and the topography of the site, the final result is open to interpretations. At first glance, the building is a traditional volume, but its lack of superfluous details ties us to and protects us from its environment, as it attempts to avoid the gray areas of nostalgia and convention.

Chun Residence

Levels of Introversion

CHUN STUDIO
COLLABORATORS: Jamie BUSH, Jon BRODY
PHOTO: ©Tim Street-Porter

SANTA MONICA – CALIFORNIA – 2003

This residence with an H-shaped layout features a two-story bar construction facing the street that acts as a monument-like wall so as to grant the residents privacy from passersby. However, for the visitor, gazing out from the inside, it would seem to dissolve as if there is a two-story void in the middle. This functions as a transition between the opaque exterior, with its heavy use of stone, and the transparency of the interior spaces that are fashioned from glass and wood.

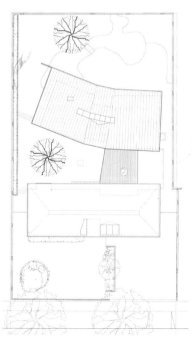

The project attempts to create its own unique world, controlled and removed from what is going on around it. The visitors' senses experience a transition as they move from the life-size, monument-evoking walls outside to the interior spaces and interior gardens. A second transition, an even larger step forward than the previous, is attained by way of the dialogue between the glassy interiors and the gardens, especially the Japanese garden.

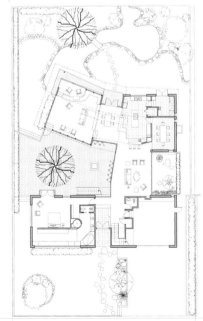

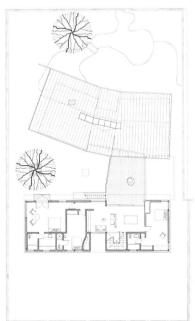

The interior of the building unfolds for the visitor where the kitchen acts as the hub for all of the other rooms. Thanks to the abundant use of glass for the interior walls, the space would appear to expand out progressively from the center to reach out finally to the garden, which instills the visitor with a sense of lightness, peace, and silence.

Island House

Limiting Nature

ARKITEKTSTUDIO WIDJEDAL RACKI BERGERHOFF
PHOTO: ©Ake Eriksson-Lindman

STOCKHOLM – SWEDEN – 2002

The house is situated on the coast of one of the islands of the Stockholm archipelago. The rather barren land features sculpturelike rocks and oak and pine trees. An oak that is believed to be 500 years old is the centerpiece of the upper part of the terrain.

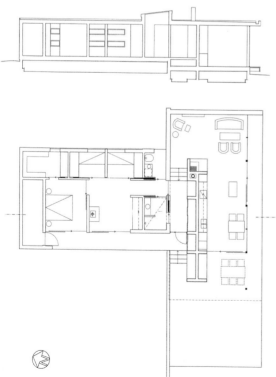

The residents, a couple with two small children, wanted the house to take full advantage of the magnificent panorama yet remain architecturally discreet. Likewise, the home was meant to be a place of comfort and relaxation as well as a place for entertaining guests.

The house is placed slightly back and slightly raised from the coastline. Hidden among the tree trunks, with an open area of terraces, it faces the ocean. The volume consists of a platform, the roof, and several common rooms with sliding doors. The more private chambers are to the rear, facing the woods among the rocks and the centuries-old oak.

02

Changing
Wood

A construction is normally considered to be something fixed and unchanging. The following projects exploit the versatility of wood. They are spaces that can undergo transformation; they are images created by wood that change with the passage of time, the seasons, the intensity of the sunlight, the inhabitation of the house, or the use of the building.

Suitcase House Hotel

Versatile Sensation

EDGE DESIGN INSTITUTE LTD.
COLLABORATORS: Andrew HOLT, Howard CHANG,
Popeye TSANG, Yee LEE
PHOTO: ©Asakawa Satoshi, Howard Chang, Gary Chang

BADALING SHUIGUAN – BEIJING– CHINA – 2001

This project was part of a competition for twelve young promising Asian architects, which entailed the design of twelve communitarian residences at the foot of the Great Wall. The proposal was for a clear and pure volume with levels inside. It needed to be extremely adaptable to diverse uses during the day, including use as a leisure space where wood would become the unifying element.

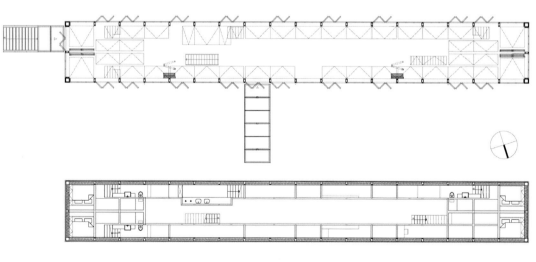

Consisting of three levels, the interior space is very malleable to diverse uses. During the day the upper level opens completely and evokes the sensation of an open hall of 144 feet in length. Later, this same area can be divided into smaller spaces for listening to music, reading, meditating, bathing, or having a sauna. Later in the day, with the arrival of more residents, the space can be reopened, or it can be made ready for sleeping.

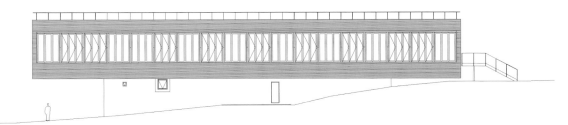

As a reflection of the free internal distribution, the facade consists of series of identical windows, like a wrapping of vertical layers, which gives a sensation of exterior uniformity while the internal organization is undergoing constant change. The interior, the furniture, the structure, and all of the elements are clad with wood, which diffuses and softens the limits of the house.

Putney House
Double Personality

PETER TONKIN, BRIAN ZULAIKHA, TIM GREER/
TONKIN ZULAIKHA GREER ARCHITECTS
PHOTO: ©Patrick Bingham Hall

SYDNEY – AUSTRALIA – 2001

As it dares to break with the passivity and uniformity of its urban setting, this expressive, playful, contained, and classical dwelling proudly rises up. On the banks of the Parramatta River in the Bay of Sydney, the light of the north and the darkness of the south define the duality of its forms, which are both open and timid, as it happily smiles to the north and politely bows to the south.

Different living rooms open out onto a courtyard that conforms the house on the north side of the bank, the largest being of double height. The south side has access to three halls so that one has the sensation of being in a classical villa. A kind of back porch provides access to the floor above where the main bedrooms and studio are located.

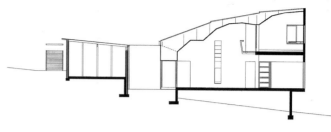

The roof facing the north draws triangles, which contrast with the straight, uniform horizontality of the opposite facade. The vertices pointing up, drawn by the wood-clad roof, provide shade for the house. Frameless windows subtly placed in the walls allow the exterior landscape scenes to be enjoyed from within.

Maison Pléneuf-Val-André

Between Presence and Absence

DAUFRESNE, LE GARREC ET ASSOCIÉS
COLLABORATORS: Eco-Bois, Gildes DARRAS
PHOTO: ©Stephen Lucas

ITÚ – FRANCE – 2002

Undertaken in two phases, first was the guest house—a discreet yet no less complete project. Phase two was the more complete project involving the main residence. Nonetheless, the two buildings really can be seen as one unitary project of mutual interdependence where the terrace, a kind of platform atop the terrain, is the hub.

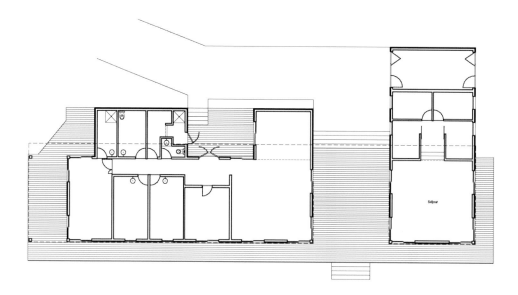

A residence that is not in constant use can pose the following dilemma; when occupied it must open out to the surrounding environment, be permeable, and let the sun in, but when not in use it should not take on the appearance of being abandoned and should be protected from the outside elements. The solution was to have moving facades that could be opened and closed at will to create a permeable, open dwelling or an impenetrable massive monolith.

The need for quick construction and the desire to coalesce the house with its setting dictated the use of kerto, fir, and coumarou wood, which resulted in very harmonious aesthetics. With an eye on practicality, the service rooms such as the kitchen and bathrooms are oriented to the north and the bedrooms, the common areas, and the terraces to the south so that the light shining in through the large windows can reach to the back of the house.

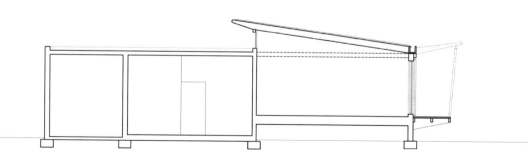

Haus Nenning

Contextual and Adaptable

CUKROWICZ.NACHBAUR ARCHITEKTEN
COLLABORATORS: Christian MOONSBRUGGER,
Saskia JÄGER, Marcus CUKROWICZ
PHOTO: ©Hanspeter Schiess Fotografie

HITTISAU – SWITZERLAND – 2002

Built by and for a carpenter, the building sits alone next to the church on the main street of a village. The plan includes three floors. The ground floor has a small shop, common areas, and entrances. The two floors above, oriented towards the south, house the family residence. Facing the north and separated by the stairwell, there is an independent yet integrated apartment for housing different generations of the family.

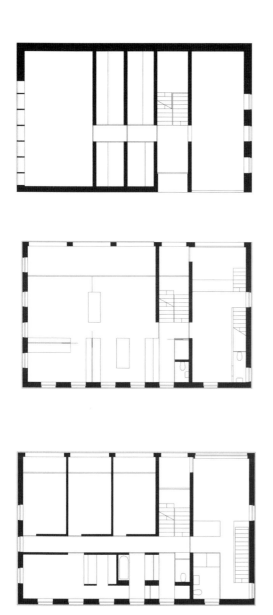

The slight variations on the facade and the sliding shutters provide protection from inclement weather. The house acquires a distinct flavor due to details in the formal composition and the use of solid wood in the construction. Variations in the size of the openings are easily attainable thanks to the sliding shutters.

Though a three-story wood house is typical of this area, this house evokes a unique character without being brazen. It fits in beautifully with its surroundings and is striking only if the observer decides to contemplate it for a second time.

03

Expert
Wood

There are occasions when the designer and the woodworker join hands, and the result of these collaborations are projects where both space and materials are dealt with the same expertise and finesse. Though sited at very different places, the executions of the following four projects reflect this because they have innovated, recuperated, or systematized, or simply because they have employed wood in a highly expert way.

Casa Dmac

Knowing the Material

NASSAR ARQUITECTES S.L.
COLLABORATORS: Domingo GONZÁLEZ,
Joaquim BALLARÍN
PHOTO: ©Daniel Nassar

VALLROMANES – BARCELONA – SPAIN – 2002

The project is conceived with a very linear orientation in mind. It divides up the terrain and opens out to the south to soak in the vistas and the light. The north side is completely closed except for the entrance. Taking advantage of a natural slope, the entrance leads directly to the second floor, which is used as common areas. The bottom floor, in direct contact with the terrain, is then reserved for the more private rooms.

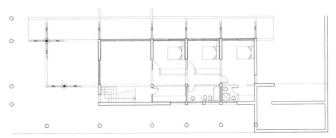

The terrace brings to mind the deck of a ship. The layout of the pavement and the lines on the wall that fade into the distance trace the beams on the ship's deck. The living room stands out on the facade and breaks the continuity of the terrace and the deck. The entrance to the house is parallel to a rough stone wall which delimits the exterior but, thanks to the front, is endowed with an open character.

The fact that the dividing walls do not reach all the way up to the ceiling highlights the continuity of space and affords ample vision of the roof structure even from the most remote corners. The careful placement of the girders and the striking use of metal tie rods is a delight. The stairs consist of a metal structure painted in white and clad with solid, white-lacquered wood, which is up against a white brick wall, thus structurally connecting the wood and the bricks.

Danielson House
Naval Construction

MACKAY-LYONS ARCHITECTS LTD.
COLLABORATORS: Trevor DAVIES, Bruno WEBER, Darryl JONAS
PHOTO: ©Undine Pröhl

SMELT BROOK – NOVA SCOTIA – CANADA – 1998

Placed on the edge of a cliff, this house was built on a modest budget for a meteorologist and a landscape painter couple. The isolation and the clear functional program are representative of an attitude and a lifestyle that has become ever more popular and is the response to the everyday absurdity of our society.

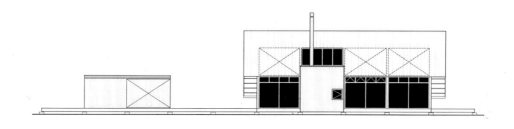

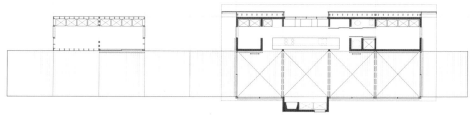

The project consists of two volumes placed atop a wooden platform, which establishes a horizontal relationship with the sea. The service areas are situated laterally and there is an open space between this area and the other so that when the weather permits, the living areas may be opened also to take advantage of this space.

In order to make the most of the available budget, prefabrication and assembly in the workshop are profusely used. Likewise, laminated wood cross-sections and wooden girders and pillars with diverse textures and finishes give it a high degree of aesthetic expressiveness. The result is a building that is like a vessel with a light and mobile structure whose habitat could be the land, water, or ice.

Mountview Residence

Recuperated Environment

JOHN MAINWARING/JMA ARCHITECTS QLD
COLLABORATORS: Jo CASE, Steve GUTHRIE
PHOTO: ©John Mainwaring, Peter Hyatt

KENILWORTH – SUNSHINE COAST - AUSTRALIA - 2001

Mountview is the reinterpretation of a way of life of bygone years and the paradigm of a landscape that refuses to disappear. The project consists of the construction and remodeling of several buildings to convey an image akin to a rural colony where different buildings are placed on the terrain haphazardly to respect and unite with the environment.

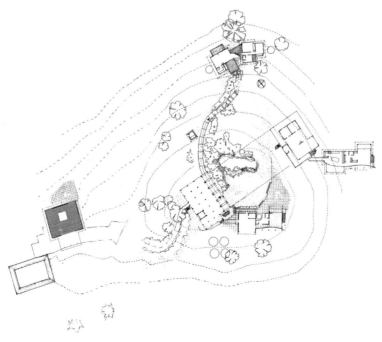

Termites destroyed much of the original woodwork dating from 1890. The rehabilitation meant minimal changes to the exterior of the building; the interior modifications are more striking. Most of the interior dividing walls were eliminated and replaced with sliding ones with louvers and all of the interior was refinished.

The apertures on both facades, large windows, and the new roofs were chosen to provide ventilation in the summer and to transform the house into a greenhouse in the winter. After the reconstruction, the interiors are open, airy, and endowed with vistas. This is a radical change from the original design fashioned to protect it from the exterior.

KFN-Pilotproject

Wood System

JOHANNES KAUFMANN AND OSKAR LEO KAUFMANN/
JOHANNES KAUFMANN ARCHITEKTUR
PHOTO: ©Ignacio Martínez

ANDELSBUCH – AUSTRIA – 1997

This house for two families is in fact a pilot project for the KFN system, which stems from the collaboration between architects and a carpenter's workshop in order to make buildings from a system of fixed modules. The modules are 16 x 16 feet with facades of 9 feet and can be placed and combined with great freedom, including wet zones such as kitchen and baths, up to a total of 24 modules.

While the architects draw up the plans in their offices, the modules and other parts are manufactured in the workshop and the foundations are laid at the site. The "kits" are then delivered to the site and assembled, as if they were a child's toy to be put together. This process guarantees reduced construction time and costs while providing an aesthetically pleasing and comfortable home.

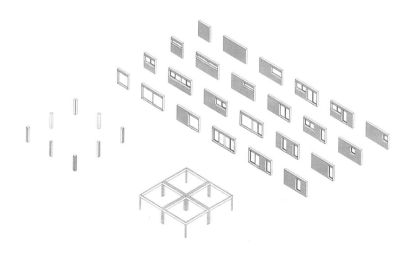

The framework of the house is made of spruce whereas the other facade and interior modules can be in any type of finish, though wood panels or plywood are preferred. The system includes other environmentally friendly features such as radiant-floor heating and recycled wood-burning heaters. The simplicity of execution is akin to the log cabin but with greater attention to design.

04

Wood
and Nature

Unlike with other materials, construction with wood allows for a harmony with nature in which there are neither winners nor losers. In the following four projects characterized by great respect for nature, the environment dictates the limit for the construction instead of being spoiled by it.

Chilmark Residence

A Clearing in the Woods

CHARLES ROSE ARCHITECTS INC.
PHOTO: ©Chuck Choi Architectural Photography

CHILMARK – MASSACHUSETTS – 2001

The site chosen by the proprietor turned out to be a true challenge. A small clearing in the woods of nonuniform dimensions obliged the layout to adapt to the scant space left free by the luxuriant vegetation. During the construction, strict measures were taken to assure that the environment was not harmed.

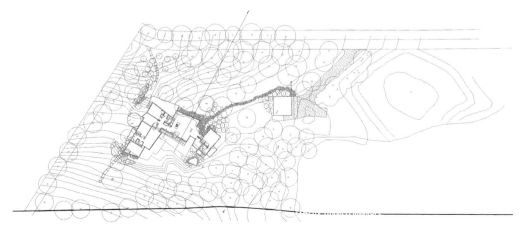

The house is laid out in three parts where a large room joins the master bedroom with the wing for the guests, which can be closed off when not in use. At the center of the house is the only modern space where the use of cedar provides abundant warm light. This area houses the living room, dining room, and kitchen.

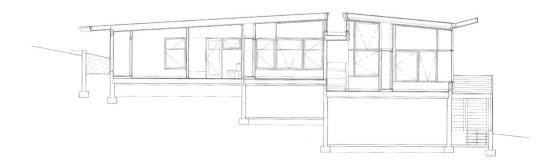

The elliptical pillars in the interior and the large sliding doors make dividing walls unnecessary. The residents can connect the space of the house to the woodsy landscape and the ocean that lies below. The terraces and the roof enhance this sense of eliminating the barriers between interior and exterior.

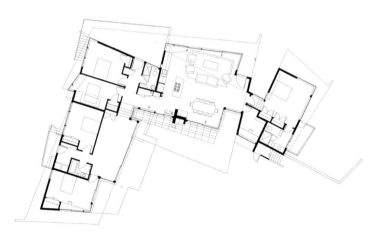

Villa Långbo

Limiting Nature

OLAVI KOPONEN ARCHITECT
COLLABORATORS: Oscari LAUKKANEN
PHOTO: ©Jussi Tianien

LÅNGHOLMEN – KEMIÖ – FINLAND – 2000

Located on the far western end of the island and exposed to the winds, this house sits at the edge of the woods. It can be partially seen from the sea, and the residents can enjoy the view of the ocean from any room. Originally built as part of a farm, some of the rooms can be converted into areas for storage or production.

Built with the idea to limit the impact of man on the environment, the building eliminates the barrier between the construction and the setting. The different enclosures, which are defined individually in relation to light, sensation, and the connection with nature, include both private and common areas and are distributed throughout a platform under a roof. The simple structure easily affords variation in the layout.

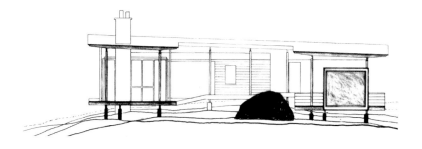

Due to periods when the ocean is frozen, it is not always possible to gain access to the building. There are times during the year when it can be reached only by using skis or boats. All of the materials utilized are recyclable and the wood comes from the immediate surroundings. All construction was done manually. The materials were transported there by horse and the setting altered as little as possible.

Koehler Retreat

Eagle's Nest

DAVID SALMELA AND SOULIYAHN KEOBOUNPHENG/
SALMELA ARCHITECTURE & DESIGN
PHOTO: ©Peter Bastianelli-Kerze

SILVER BAY – MINNESOTA – 2003

Fleeing from modernity without renouncing its concepts, this dwelling was built on the wildest and most daring edge of nature. It is located atop a precipice with a spectacular view of Lake Superior.

The bark from the surrounding cherry, maple, and cypress trees decorates the interior and exterior of the house. Maple is used for the windows, ceilings, stairs, and closets whereas maple and cherry are used for the floors. The facade of recycled cypress is a continuation of the landscape that surrounds it, together with the laminated wood beams that connect the house to its solid rock roots.

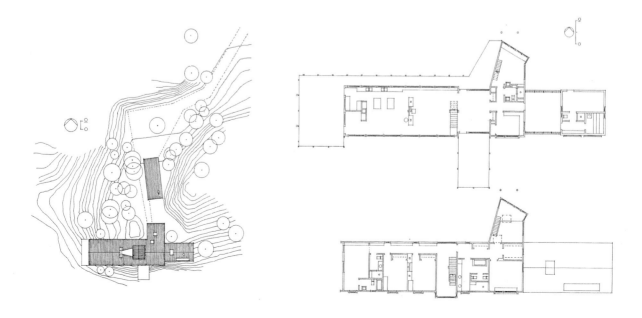

The empty, nude interior eagerly awaits the coming of the first rays of the sun and the shadows of the trees. The more often used areas of the house are privileged with direct sunlight whereas the studio where the artist works receives more filtered and subdued light. The textures of the wood and the chiaroscuro of the passing day attest to the beauty of this sheltered dwelling in the midst of nature.

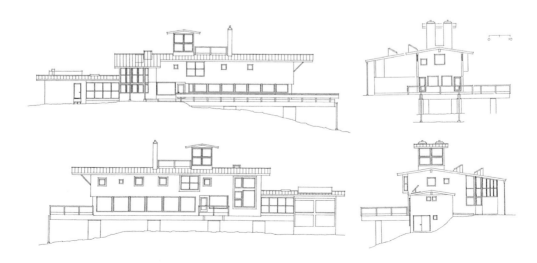

Casa Acayaba

Arboreal Life

MARCOS ACAYABA ARQUITETOS SC LTDA
COLLABORATORS: Mauro HALLULI, Suely MIZOBE,
Fabio VALENTIM
PHOTO: ©Nelson Kon

TIJUCOPAVA – GUARAJÁ – BRAZIL – 1997

This house is a model for constructing on slopes without harming the environment. Though only 490 feet from the beach, it is 230 feet above sea level. Placed in the midst of the woods on the Atlantic coast, the foundation consists of only three pillars placed among the trees, which create a hexagon. The triangular structure, which spreads out like another tree, is fit together with wood pillars and beams, steel, cables, and turnbuckles.

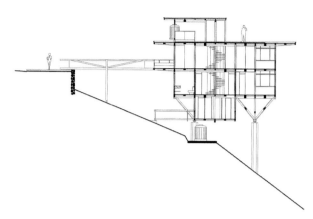

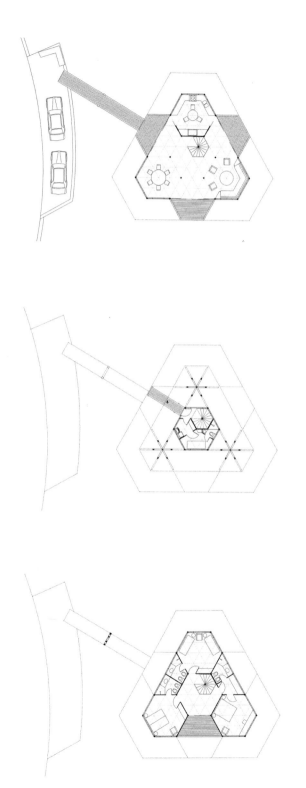

The deck, with protection from the tropical rains, is like an open-air living room. There, at the top of the trees, the residents can enjoy the views of the surrounding hills and the ocean. An independent pathway provides access to the main floor, which houses the common areas and the kitchen. The bedrooms are located on the upper floor, and the lower floor houses the service areas.

The concept was to fashion the different light construction pieces in the workshop, which allowed the entire building to be constructed in four months by only four people with minimal impact on the surrounding environment. The triangular geometry of the structure, rigid by nature, creates greater communication of the spaces with the exterior, as the facade gives the sensation of a series of balconies.

05

Wood
in the Skin

At times the value of wood does not lie in its strength or load-bearing qualities. The following four projects of distinct origins demonstrate how wood can enrich the visual aesthetics of a building as well.

Eave House

Protective Overhang

KAHARU AND YUI TEZUKA/TEZUKA ARCHITECTS
AND MASAHIRO IKEDA
PHOTO: ©Katsuhisa Kida

TOKYO – JAPAN – 2002

The monsoon that starts at the beginning of June and envelopes the city of Tokyo for one month strongly marks the character of this house. During this hot season of heavy rains, the interior of homes need refreshing gusts of wind and at the same time protection from the rainwater. A sixteen-feet eave around the open areas of the residence attempts to solve this problem posed by the climate.

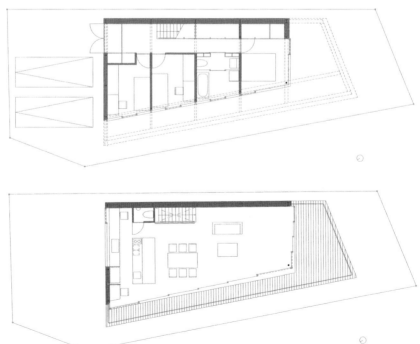

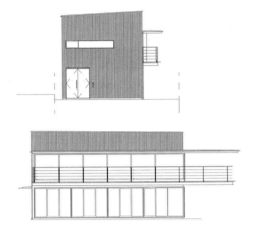

The intermediate space of the house provides a height of slight dimensions in order to control the influx of direct sunlight and splashing from the rain. A pillar situated at the most open corner of the facade becomes open to the sky when the sliding doors are drawn, which lengthens the interior space and extends it to the edge of the eave outside.

Mehrfamilienhaus II

New in the Neighborhood

VOGT ARCHITEKTEN ETH SIA
COLLABORATORS: Marcel KNOBLANCH, Antonella SILENO,
Marc LIECHTI
PHOTO: ©Dominic Büttner

MUHEN – SWITZERLAND – 2004

The setting is the principal compositional element for this apartment block. It is
placed in a neighborhood whose hub is a country house dating from 1813. By way
of contemporary art language, which makes use of local materials and sensible
volumes, it proposes the integration and assimilation with a consolidated setting.

The building houses four small apartments of two different types. The facade is a skin of untreated larch panels, which is the local wood. The volume and the facade grant an assimilation between the small buildings in the setting.

Wood is of special importance in the facades and balconies, where it is used in a separate metal structure, and in the stairwell with the steps that combine glass block and reinforced concrete in a relaxing atmosphere in harmony with its semi-public use. It is also used in the parquet wood floors and for all of the furniture of the entryway and kitchen, which combines treated wood and linoleum.

Galloway Residence

Wood in Abundance

THE MILLER HULL PARTNERSHIP
COLLABORATORS: Robert HULL, Petra MICHAELY,
Brian COURT
PHOTO: ©Benjamin Benschneider

MERCER ISLAND – WASHINGTON – 2003

This residence is placed on wooded hillside that gives the impression of being terraced on the shores of Lake Washington. It is privileged with a panorama of the lake and a bridge provides access at the upper level. Once inside, a central staircase of wood, steel, and concrete descends down to the common areas on the lower floor, which open out to the shore of the lake.

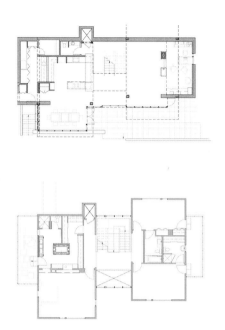

Two large boxes wrapped in wood perch atop a continuous bare cement wall. Most private areas are located on the second and third floors. A guesthouse has been designed under the roof plan. The boxes are clad with yellow cedar slats as are the base below and its sides, which give continuity to the volume.

The combination of materials used for this building are the wood covering, steel, and bare concrete, which draw the volumes with striking clarity and play with the duality of the vistas of the woods and the lake. Matte finish aluminum is used for the windows while apple wood and bamboo are the material of choice for the interiors. The central staircase is like a patio, which provides the house with good natural ventilation.

Casa en Chamartín

A Second Skin

FUENSANTA NIETO AND ENRIQUE SOBEJANO/
NIETO SOBEJANO ARQUITECTOS S.L.
COLLABORATORS: Carlos BALLESTEROS,
Mauro HERRERO, Juan Carlos REDONDO
PHOTO: ©Luis Asín, Hisao Suzuki

MADRID – SPAIN – 2002

The desire to build a new home in a residential area dating from the 1950s came up against regulations that prohibited the demolition of the original edifice. Consequently, the architects came up with an in-depth transformation along two lines: a new wooden envelope to cover all of the former building and a new "spinal column" from top to bottom of the structure.

The new envelope is a skin consisting of high-density bakelite-treated wood panels. Aluminum rails fasten it to the walls with an air chamber so that the walls become ventilated facades. The ground floor is covered with corrugated aluminum and the roof with copper.

Inside a central furniture unit, the "spinal column," concentrates a maximum number of elements that serve the main spaces: closets, bookcases, shelves, electronic devices, and diverse utility and service ducts, tubes, and pipes, thus freeing the floor space for other uses.

06

Sustainable
Wood

Wood is a material that is renewable, environmentally friendly, recyclable, and sustainable. Following are four projects that incorporate the concept of sustainability as one element in the design. Whether in Brazil or Central Europe, respect for the environment, energy conservation, and the awareness that the planet we inhabit is not limitless are now the pervasive thinking.

Casa Bandeira de Mello

Comfortable and Sustainable

MAURO MUNHOZ ARQUITETURA
COLLABORATORS: Andrea FELTRIN, Eduardo LOPES, Viviane ALVES, Fabiana TANURI
PHOTO: ©Nelson Kon

ITÚ – BRAZIL – 2003

Located twenty-five miles from Sao Paolo, this house was designed for a young couple and their two small children as a weekend retreat and also as a place to receive guests, host parties and family reunions, and as a possible permanent residence for the future. Logically, the distribution calls for two wings; one for the family and one for guests.

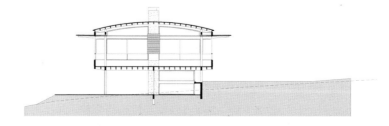

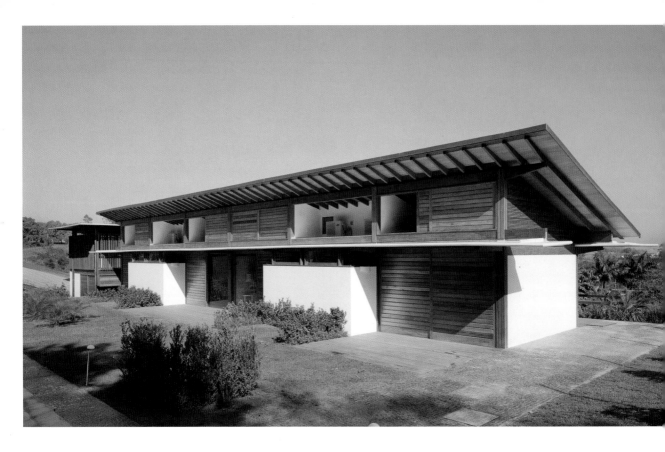

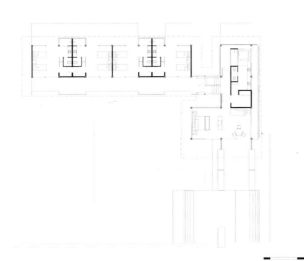

The topography comes to the fore in the project as the house is prominently visible from the street, but at the same time provides privacy to the residents. Open spaces akin to porches, such as the living room and the access to the bedrooms, can be enjoyed, thus taking full advantage of the tropical climate. When the sun flows into these intermediate spaces, it likewise generously bathes the adjacent rooms.

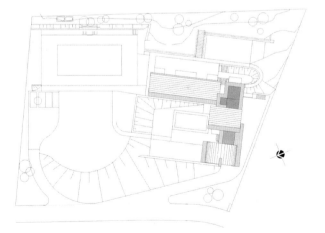

The structure of the house, totally of coumarou wood with environmental certification, was cut and prepared in workshops and assembled at the site with great speed. Features of the project design, such as passive ventilation, natural light, and the shade provided by porches and breezeways, improve the energy efficiency of the house.

Haus Steinwendtner
Divine Atmosphere

HERTL ARCHITEKTEN
COLLABORATOR: Michael SCHRÖCKENFUCHS
PHOTO: ©Paul Ott

STEYR-MÜNCHHOLZ – AUSTRIA– 2003

Designed as a low-cost one-family home, this house is totally made of wood, except for the two volumes sitting in the garden; the garage for bicycles and the garden shed, which are made of steel. To compensate for the lack of surface space, the transit areas that connect the common areas on the lower floor are integrated, which results in a floor plan without passageways.

Once inside the house, the visitor becomes aware of the general volume of the building and enjoys a feeling of spaciousness that is impossible to anticipate from the outside. Through the glass panels at the top, sunlight from the south filters in like mist into the living room areas. This blocks the view in from the street and creates an ambience of introversion.

On the north side the living room expands out to the green of the adjoining woods thanks to the terrace, which is cut from the building. The analogy of the light that floods the house, which is filtered through the trees or other rooms, to the light found in sacred places, which is distant and full of subtleties, was a premise throughout the project.

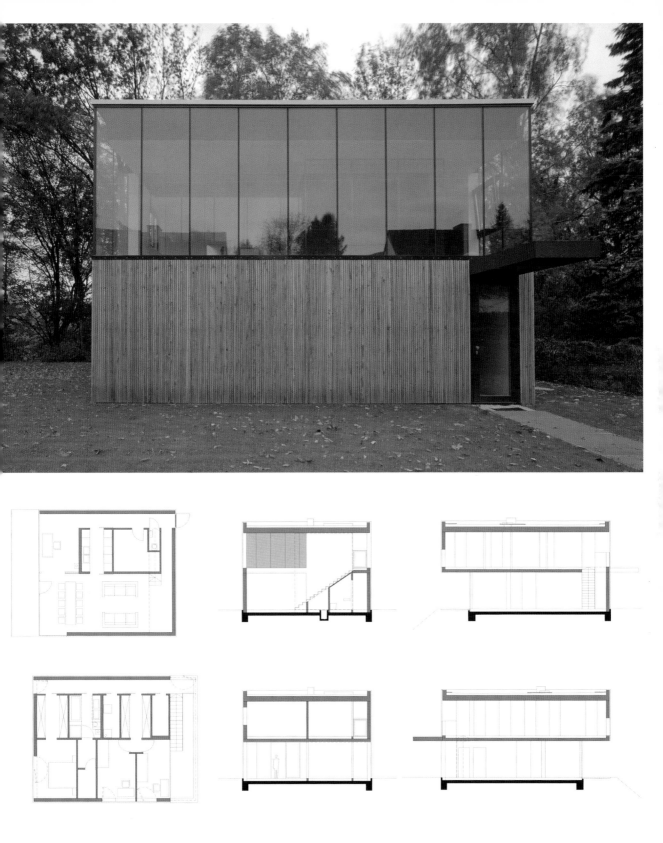

Passivehausanlage

Energy Trapper

JOHANNES KAUFMANN AND OSKAR LEO KAUFMANN/
JOHANNES KAUFMANN ARCHITEKTUR
PHOTO: ©Ignacio Martínez

DORNBIRN – AUSTRIA – 2003

The complex consists of one building and nine apartments in a row complete with
an underground garage. It is all built in wood, which is a novelty as until now fire
restrictions obliged the use of fire walls between each residence. It is part of a
much larger residential area arranged in rows. Seen in its entirety, it is a cityscape
made up of series of distinct facades.

The rational design makes use of the least possible space, thus reducing costs. The spaces are small but open and lend themselves to be redrawn according to the criteria of each homeowner. The floor plan is flexible and allows for modifications in the walls in the future.

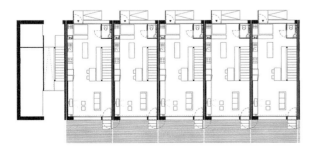

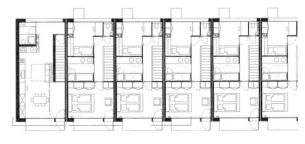

Concerns for environment are prominent in the design. The homes are perfectly insulated, the influx and outflow of air is tightly controlled, the heating is highly efficient, the glass and skylights passively capture light and energy, and the roof is ventilated. The final result is buildings whose energy costs are 60-80 percent less than the average.

Wohnhaus mit Atelier

Elegant Simplicity

THOMAS MAURER ARCHITEKT
PHOTO: ©Francesca Giovanelli

LANGENTHAL – SWITZERLAND – 2001

Designed as a family residence and an architectural studio, the architect is also the creator of this project. Located in a formerly industrialized area, it formally consists of rotund cubic wooden forms that convey elegant simplicity. The studio is situated in the basement, the common areas on the ground floor, and the bedrooms on the two upper floors with a porch at the front that grants a brushstroke of originality.

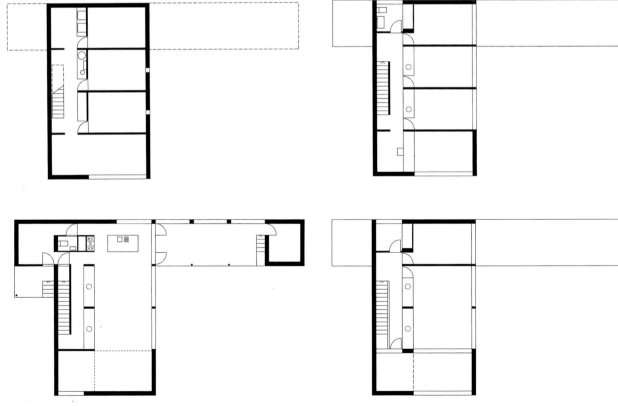

Reinforced concrete forms the base on which a building made of fir wood was built. With a clear north-south orientation, the windowless north facade is in stark contrast to the south that is completely open in order to soak in the sun. In between the two is the service zone that houses the bathroom, kitchen, and the stairs. With movable panels, the rooms can be opened up or closed off.

Built with great speed, the dwelling consists of a tough wooden structure lined with panels and covered on the outside with larch wood slats. Many energy-saving features are incorporated into the project: solar energy devices, collection and use of rainwater, and pollution-free utilization of local wood.

07

Wood
Interiors

Following are some of the vast array of possibilities for the use of wood in interior design and decoration, presented by rooms, not by projects, to facilitate comparisons and from public spaces to the more private rooms.

Great (Bamboo) Wall

KENGO KUMA & ASSOCIATES

PHOTO: © Satoshi Asakawa

A group of architects led by Kengo Kuma designed this house near the Great Wall for a competition of young talents in Asian architecture. The symbolic value of bamboo is accentuated to the limit as it is used for the walls and the partitions, filling the atmosphere with a warmth that flows out to the exterior.

Roof House

TEZUKA ARCHITECTS

PHOTO : © Katsuhisa Kida

In this house built in Kanagawa, Japan, a cyclical landscape is developed that connects the internal space of the home to the sky through skylights that can be reach by the stairs from each room. The sloped sky responds to the topography in which it is placed. The roof is inhabitable and equipped with benches, table, kitchen, and even a shower, as it is converted into yet another room in the house. It is connected to the garden by an exterior stairs.

Michaelis House

HARRY LEVINE ARCHITECTS

PHOTO: © Patrick Bingham-Hall

This residence was built in Sydney, Australia, in 2002. It boasts a spacious and inviting living room that is comfortable and replete with discreet beauty. Open, thanks to the windows running the full length of the exterior wall, there is a dialogue between the exterior red cedar, cherry, and Tasmanian oak trees and the recycled wood within, and the wise old trees filling the vistas of the nearby reserve in the Bay of Willoughby and the cliffs of Cammeray.

Treasure Palace

EDGE DESIGN INSTITUTE LTD

PHOTO: © Janet Choy, Gary Chang

This house in Taipei, Taiwan, has intelligent spaces controlled by invisible technological systems. Instead of rooms, there are different "strata" where activities are carried out according to the elements contained within. The conventional concept of living room is rejected and instead "layers" are designed according to the intended activities for that particular space. Thus, after following a cobblestone path running along the house we come upon a "green layer" where we may repose, or an "information layer" where we can feel sheltered while lounging in golden wooden boxes surrounded by books.

Maison Goulet

SAÏA BARBARESE TOPOUZANOV ARCHITECTS

Located in Québec, Canada, the wooden structure of the residence has a stone base and is strengthened by two stone chimneys, one for a rest area and one for a meeting area. The interior is completely covered with wood panels and imbues it with the same ambience as the exterior. The stretched height of the ceiling seems to reach upward like the upward growth of the trees that long to reach the sky. The width seems to spread out transparently and endlessly under the charming gaze of the forest.

Villa Långbo

OLAVI KOPONEN ARCHITECT

PHOTO: © Jussi Tiainen

Located in Finland, this house is designed to remove all barriers that could separate man from nature. The walls aspire to be transparent, with glass there only to keep out the cold. The wooden frames of the windows participate in the script of harmony composed by the outstretched rising arms of the trees. A walk around the house is to take a stroll in the woods and to sit to rest beneath the ceiling of treetops.

Chun Residence

DAVID CHUN/CHUN STUDIO

This house is located in Santa Monica, California. The interior generates reclusive spaces of calm and tranquility. By using wood and sober, warm furniture, it attempts to transpose the sensations of the exterior gardens to the interior.

Casa Acayaba

MARCOS ACAYABA ARQUITETOS SC LTDA

PHOTO: © Nelson Kon

Placed in a forest on the Atlantic coast in Brazil, this residence is designed to be yet one more tree in its setting. It is inlaid in its topography in a natural way and is the expression of continuous spaces that lead to the ocean or to the mountain range. The height, as high as that of a tree, affords incomparable and privileged repose near the treetops. The interior, which is rich in wood, is like a series of open balconies with vistas.

Casa Bandeira de Mello

MAURO MUNHOZ ARQUITETURA

This house, located in Itú, Brazil, boasts a richness of subtleties and uses for wood in the living room areas that are absolutely astonishing. Designed with open character and great spatial continuity, these common spaces feel more like terraces than closed enclosures.

Pine Forest Cabin

CUTLER ANDERSON ARCHITECTS

The small cabin designed in Washington in 1999 is an attempt to minimize its dimensions and impact on the setting to as little as possible. Bedroom, kitchen, and bathroom are grouped together in the most concealed part of the house whereas the common area, drawn as a double-height space, is totally opened out to the landscape. Fashioned with a simple facade with a wooden strut trimming, the interior space is enlarged by drawing in the participation of the exterior.

Residential in Öschingen

MARTINA SCHLUDE ARCHITEKTEN

This residential project in Germany built in 2001 is an unwavering proponent of energy conservation as it makes passive use of solar radiation. Sober yet inviting interiors are achieved by means of simple and compact volumes, restrained pure lines, and rigorous approach to construction. The abundant use of wood is noteworthy because it is supplied in sustainable and ecological way and can also be recycled.

Wohnhaus Stuttgart

MARTINA SCHLUDE ARCHITEKTEN

PHOTO : © Juraj Liptak, Reiner Blunk

This chalet in Germany is privileged with a large, spacious multifunctional space that can be redrawn at will, thanks to movable panels. The filtered light that flows in all throughout the day diffuses into a wide range of transparencies and intimacy and is fragmented by the slats of the shades. The wood intervenes in the diverse shades of transparency as it filters the exterior light while the steps of the stairs gently stroke it.

Chalet Pictet

CHARLES PICTET ARCHITEKT FAS SIA

PHOTO: © Francesca Giovanelli

This house, built in the Swiss Alps in 1872 and fashioned from logs, was restored and enlarged in 2000. It concentrates in its interior the slow passing of time like the drops of a gentle yet perennial rain. The oldness and aging is incorporated into the contemporaneity of the house where the patina of aging wood is in harmony with the youthful emotions of recently cut wood. The skillful hands of yesteryear are fused with the rhythmic beat of the present. The wood, warm and friendly, dominates in this atmosphere of thick walls.

Duplex rue de Savoie

LITTOW ARCHITECTES

The remodeling of this attic apartment in Paris in 2004 restored the original character of the wood by eliminating all posterior additions or modifications from the original. The wood ceiling sways like the waves of the sea as it gives off waves of calm that gently rock the land that sustains it. The horizons are vertically connected by way of the wooden bars that separate two differentiated spaces.

Mehrfamilienhaus II

VOGT ARCHITEKTEN

PHOTO: © Dominic Büttner

Pantries and cabinets, which combine a wide range of dark shades of wood and linoleum with a parquet floor as a backdrop, make up this sober and elegant kitchen that is so neat and prim that it seems not ready for cooking but rather for a party.

Chalet Pictet

CHARLES PICTET ARCHITEKT FAS SIA

PHOTO: © Francesca Giovanelli

This kitchen in a restored residence is wrapped in wood and feels like an island where the passing of time seems of little concern. The heat from simmering dishes and the aromas of slowly cooking food always seem to permeate the solid rotund walls with their watchful eyes.

Latorre Residence

GARY CUNNINGHAM ARCHITECT

This Dallas home presents an agile and contemporary kitchen made up of compact modules that convey a sense of efficiency, but also a ironic playfulness as exemplified by the use of the spotlights. The wooden beams that support the ceiling form an integral part of the space as shelves and other kitchen utensils are hung from them.

Wood House

CUTTLER ANDERSON ARCHITECTS

PHOTO: © Undine Pröhl

This kitchen is located at the back of a continuously unbroken shared space that houses the living room and dining room. The space gives off two different ambiences, which the fireplace fills with warmth. A walk in it is like penetrating the depths of a forest with a wide variety of trees. The cabinets seem to be the refuge for birds and the beams seem to be patiently awaiting the flight of a bird while time placidly and calmly passes by among warm colors and soft lights.

Michaelis House

HARRY LEVINE ARCHITECTS

Situated in a residence in Australia, a bar of cabinets and shelves made of wood frame the picture that is the passageway of the kitchen. The windows that provide it with ample natural sunlight are also used to support shelves that display everyday objects for use in the kitchen.

Maison Goulet

SAÏA BARBARESE TOPOUZANOV ARCHITECTS

PHOTO: © Marc Cramer

The abundant use of wood panels for the walls is of special interest here. A stone wall opens up to give entry into the kitchen with a bar for guests. It is part of a long path of glass and wood throughout the house that makes the visitors feel as if they are in the middle of nature.

Island House

ARKITEKTSTUDIO WIDJEDAL RACKI BERGERHOFF

PHOTO: © Åke Erikson Lindman

The kitchen is an essential meeting place and the residents can gaze out its window to the ocean, among locks of hair made of oak trees and the silhouettes of rocks. Built in and melded with the wall and the wood that clads all of the house, it is discreet and silently elegant.

Studio 3773

DRY DESIGN

PHOTO: © Undine Pröhl

In tight spaces, such as this residence in Los Angeles, California, ingenuity is needed in order to make maximum use of available space. The solution for the bedroom in this small home is to fashion a small loft over the living room area, half-hidden among the structural beams. This pleasant and cheerful intervention enriches the space with the presence of wood that is skillfully elaborated.

Duplex rue de Savoie

LITTOW ARCHITECTES

The remodeling of this attic apartment in Paris allowed the bedroom to be placed directly beneath the roof. The wood structure was stripped and restored, which grants warmth to the space. There is an overall sense that everything is provisional, which is accentuated with the placement of the bed; directly on the floor, almost monastic, and illuminated by the windows overhead.

Chalet Pictet

CHARLES PICTET ARCHITEKT FAS SIA

PHOTO: ©Francesca Giovanelli

Three bedrooms in the same house exemplify three different and distinct uses for wood. Present is sinuous wood for dressing a wall, which is both functional and decorative, a mosaic of circular forms drawn by the grains and tones of the material. There is aged and aging wood whose rustic presence is humble and simple. And there is wood adapted to modernity. Taken in its entirety, all three uses creates simplicity and transforms the interior into a unique space.

Treasure Palace

EDGE DESIGN INSTITUTE LTD

PHOTO: ©Janet Choy, Gary Chang

The approach to decorating this bedroom is akin to the way interiors are designed in the Far East. A strict plan distributes the dorm in continuity so that it is the furniture that defines the spaces more than the walls. This premise is taken to the extreme as even the wall that separates the bedroom from the hallway becomes simply a formal limit as it is made of fillets that allow light to flow in.

Maison Goulet

SAÏA BARBARESE TOPOUZANOV ARCHITECTS

PHOTO: © Marc Cramer

A simple geometric volume totally lacking in details is the domain of this bedroom. It is on display in the center of a wooden box and tiny apertures of light slice the immensity of what surrounds it outside. The bed, bathed in serenity and quiet, is the only object that hints of the function of this room. At the same time, an unending dialogue of silence with the setting of hefty trunks continues on and on.

Flooded House

GAD ARCHITECTURE

PHOTO: © Ali Bekman, Salih Kucuktuna

The signs of the cultures, separated by centuries but also very distinct, which now make up the riches of the city of Istanbul, can be found in these bedrooms; a bed that reposes beneath the frame of an Ottoman house, and another that snuggles up against a wall and has seen the sleeping and the awakening of three different generations.

House with Three Eras

House in Finland

WOOD FOCUS FINLAND

PHOTO: © Esko Jåmså, Mikko Auerniitty

In one of the bedrooms in this house in Finland, completed in 2002, the walls and the ceiling are made with sheets of wood painted in blue to convey a marine ambience. Being in a meeting point is the sensation in this room thanks to the criss-cross of vertical and horizontal lines stemming from the furniture and layout.

Treasure Palace

EDGE DESIGN INSTITUTE LTD

PHOTO: ©Janet Choy, Gary Chang

In one of the corners of this immense field of comfort and pleasure, midst the rich wood shining in all of its golden splendor, is the bathroom. It is one of the best kept treasures of this house. Here, there are just the right number of objects, all ideally placed, to maximize the aesthetics of the different lines.

Suitcase House Hotel

EDGE DESIGN INSTITUTE LTD

PHOTO: ©Asakawa Satoshi,
Howard Chang, Gary Chang

Semiunderground in a large continuous space of this changeable house designed
next to the Great Wall of China, the visitors are only given a clue as to the presence
of the bathroom. It appears and disappears under a floor of wooden doors that
open and close to afford the necessary privacy or to provide a new ambience.

Casa Bandeira de Mello

MAURO MUNHOZ ARQUITETURA

Thanks to the topographical characteristics of the setting where Casa Bandeira de Mello is located, its bathroom with large windows can be thoroughly enjoyed. Its simplicity and warmth contrasts with the soberness and introversion of Island House, which only unveils its privacy with elegant discretion to the skies of Sweden.

Island House

ARKITEKTSTUDIO WIDJEDAL RACKI BERGERHOFF

House with Three Eras

GAD ARCHITECTURE

Stone, earth, wood, bricks, and concrete fill this bathroom with autumn hues, grooves, and lines, which create a field of extensive spaces for minimal objects hanging in the air. The ambience of this enclosure is a composition consisting of a mosaic of geometric layers of different materials and colors. Without taking prominence, the wood appears striking at times and is well coordinated with the other materials.

House R.

WOLFGANG FEYFERUK/SUSI FRITZER ARCHITEKTEN

PHOTO: © Paul Ott. Graz

Interior bathrooms are often dark and claustrophobic spaces. In this project completed in Austria in 2002, these problems were overcome by replacing walls with shelves, which allows the exterior light to flow in. By strategically placing the books, the residents can satisfy their needs for more or less privacy or light. To contrast with the wood, white ceramic bathroom fixtures are used.

House in Finland

WOOD FOCUS FINLAND

PHOTO: © Esko Jåmså, Mikko Auerniitty

Upon entering this space our attention is drawn to the wooden sauna; we are beckoned to enter its calm and warm interior as we open the doors that continue the harmony created by the bathroom. Once again, the hues of the wood combine perfectly with the white bathroom fixtures. The windows grant a feeling of spaciousness.

Chalet Pictet

CHARLES PICTET ARCHITEKT FAS SIA

PHOTO: © Francesca Giovanelli

Once again in the remodeling of this house in the Swiss Alps, the warm hues and soft texture of the smooth wood, present before the restoration, contrast with the roughness of the grayish stone, which strikingly accentuates the warmth of the bathroom.

Porch House

TEZUKA ARCHITECTS

PHOTO: © Katsuhisa Kida

Exterior is interior, and interior is exterior. All of the house is one huge porch which brings the setting in closer to us. A gust of wind is the oxygen that the inhabitants breathe, and sunlight is the light that paints the chiaroscuro of the nooks and crannies. To live in this house is to be in the open air without feeling cold or hot, to snuggle up under the stars and to bathe in the rain.

Avalon House

CONNOR + SOLOMON ARCHITECTS

This house, built in Australia in 2003, is a poignant example of how a small terrace is efficiently used. A narrow terrace gains in prominence thanks to the transparent facade, which broadens it while expanding the interior. A large surface that runs the breadth of the house, slightly elevated from the ground, creates inviting spaces for the home in close harmony with the setting.

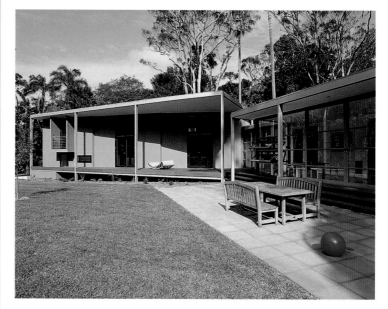

Haus Nenning

CUKROWICZ.NACHBAUR ARCHITEKTEN

In this residence, built in Austria in 2004, the exterior space is contained in a box with transparent doors and wood frame windows, which allows in flashes and streaks of changing light throughout the day. The windows and doors open up like a shop window to generously display all that can not be bought, but can only be given away. The wood colors the intermediate ambience with warm light.

Haus Hein

CUKROWICZ.NACHBAUR ARCHITEKTEN

This house of traditional aesthetics was given a contemporary twist thanks to the platform that launches the admirer towards the vistas. The terrace represents a horizontal line on the verticality of the building. There is a corner with a roof overhead and a balcony that seems to hold up the sky. The floor is a continuous line that directs the gaze out to the horizon. It is a king's seat overlooking a stage with the mountains as the protagonists, which seem to be distancing themselves but never completely disappear.

Flooded House

GAD ARCHITECTURE

PHOTO: © Ali Bekman, Salih Kucuktuna

Built on the banks of the Bosporus between Europe and Asia, this house is a reminder of the splendor of the Ottoman period. It sits between two seas and two continents and among centuries of history and centuries of history to come. The terrace and the porch are a calm space for witnessing the navigation in the strait. That same water, so near and unable to be duly contained in the underground pool, causes the seepage into the interior of the building.

Great (Bamboo) Wall

KENGO KUMA & ASSOCIATES

The subtlety of bamboo and the symbolism it holds for the cultural exchange between China and Japan are a bridge that penetrates even the Great Wall. The interconnected rods of bamboo are joined to delimit the exterior of the house. Inside, it is restrained, like brushstrokes that are trapped on white paper, without obstacles or depth.

Matthews Residence

JMA ARCHITECTS QLD

PHOTO: © John Mainwaring

The construction of this house in Bardon, Australia was completed in 2002. It is embellished with two balconies that project out, which are beautifully braced by two slanted pillars. This feature suggests that the balconies are being tossed back into the forest that surrounds the house, thus returning to their place of origin.

08

To Have
a Dream

After an eventful journey, we return to our starting point: wood on wood. Tree houses make our childhood dreams of independence, secret hideouts, and contact with nature come true. Here are three examples: one is clearly dreamlike, the second is rationally entertaining, and the third is practically residential .

Paul Mead Tree House

New Life

THOMAS HOWARD, TOMAS MILLAR, JAMES FOOTTIT
PHOTO: © Melissa Moore

BISLEY – GLOUCESTERSHIRE – UNITED KINGDOM – 2003

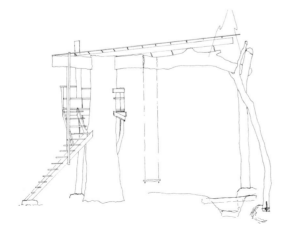

The ideas that guide the premise of this project are to recuperate an old oak tree, which can now only offer its skeleton, and to inject new life into its remains without tearing it out from the ground. It is designed mainly with children and their grandmother in mind. The tree trunk becomes the pillar that holds up a volatile place, a refuge of tales and long-lost sensations.

A small house, barely enclosed with a railing and covered with a scanty parasol, was designed at the top of a staircase. It is a runway where dreams can take flight. Though built without walls, the roof is broad enough to provide protection from the rain. The interior grants sufficient space to accommodate impromptu visits.

With the passing of time the newly planted elm beside it will grow branches towards and around the house. Blossoms and flowers will cover it with color, smell, and new life. The birds are already building their nests in it. The sea of vegetation at the base is creating the necessary image of mystery and distance from the garden. A swing hangs from one of the branches.

1:50

Lee Tree House

Negotiating Living Together

JOSEPH LIM ARCHITECT
COLLABORATORS: C.I. YEO, Lai Wai HENG
PHOTO: © Ismurnee Khayon

GALLOP PARK – SINGAPORE – 2002

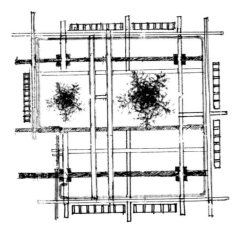

For this project a metal and wood structure that totally bears in mind the role of the two trees is of utmost importance. The trees impose their rules and these must be religiously respected. The first step was the thorough study of the trees.

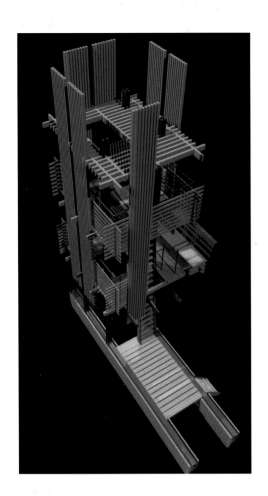

The trees must be thoroughly and precisely mapped to decide on the basic points of support so that the tree house can "sprout" from the dead trunks, thus breathing life into it. A juxtaposition of wooden and iron bars embrace the tree to form an exquisite communion with nature, now and in the future.

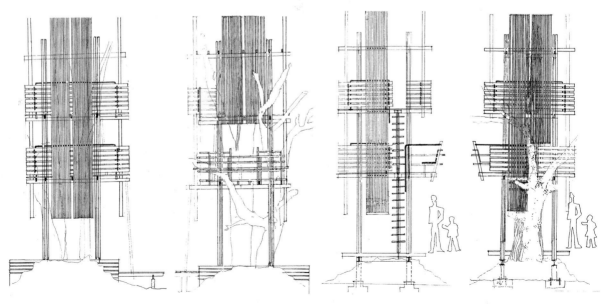

The dreams of a child, who wants to find a place in nature where he can let his imagination wander, lies in the labyrinth interiors of this house, full of secret nooks and crannies. The architect planed a reencounter with childhood and gave it a solid foundation so that the "magic carpet" can be unfolded atop the house and the visitors can begin to fly anywhere they want.

Hardy Tree House
Double Level

YEW KUAN/AREA
PHOTO : © Rio Helmi

BAUNG – BALI – 2002

To be one with nature and to become an inherent part of its meaning have been a latent desire of mankind from the beginning of time. To see the earth from a bird's-eye view, to watch the goings-on from atop a cloud, and to witness events without being seen, could all be wishes contained in this house entangled with trunks and branches.

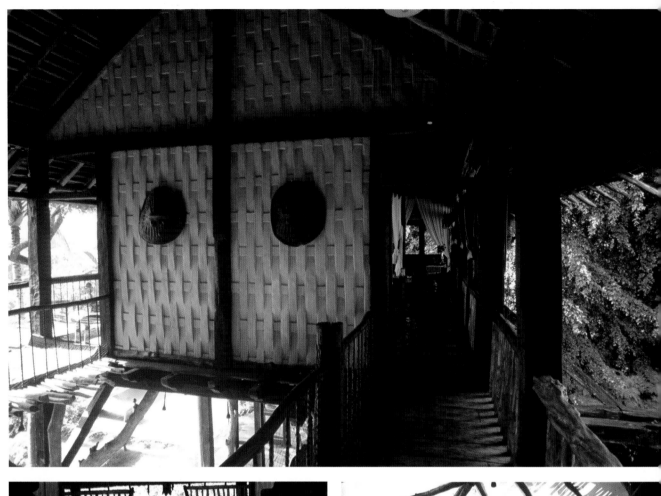

Like a mirage suspended midair, we see the elongated, horizontal body that cuts the verticality of the trees. The skeleton, made of logs and live tree branches, requires reinforcement with wooden props at certain points. A layer of subtlety seems to sustain this untamed house, which is perfectly inhabitable.

The lower floor is open with a porch, which are used as common areas. The second floor, atop the porch in fact, houses the private spaces. The subtle combination of wood tones, fabrics, and furniture in warm and toast-brown tones, endows the house with a sense of comfort.

WOOD CATALOGUE

The following is an index for different types of wood in which the appearance, nomenclature, physical properties, and uses are outlined.

GLOSSARY

· **Alburnum** (or sapwood): The part of the tree with living cells that transports or stores nutrients. It is a lighter color and more porous than the duramen, and can rot.

· **Duramen** (or heartwood): The mature part of the wood that is the structural part of the tree. It is without living cells.

Microscopic Characteristics

· **Grain:** The direction of the wood fibers in respect to the axis of the tree. Straight grain wood, parallel to the axis, is easy to work with. Wavy, curved, spiral or slanted grain is more difficult to work with, but aesthetically affords more possibilities.

Physical Characteristics

· **Density:** The relationship between mass and volume with 12% humidity, which is expressed in kg/m^3. In conifers it ranges from 400 (very light) to 700 (very heavy), and in broadleaves, from 500 to 950.

· **Hardness:** Indicates the index of penetration of one material into another and specifies the resistance of the wood to abrasion or chipping.

· **Hygroscopicity:** The capacity of the wood to absorb more or less moisture (water) from the atmosphere or from the medium that it is in.

· **Contraction:** Shrinkage due to a loss of moisture.

· **Ratio of unit volume contraction:** The change in volume that wood undergoes due to a 1% change in moisture. According to this ratio wood may have:
   Slight density (0.15-0.40), ideal for the manufacture of furniture;
   Fair density (0.35-0.49), good for carpentry;
   Average density (0.40-0.55), good for construction;
   Rather high density (0.55-0.75), good for radial construction;
   Very high density (0.75-1), ideal for environments with perpetual moisture.

Mechanical characteristics

· **Cracking or splitting:** It indicates the resistance to breakage if penetrated, nailed, or screwed into.

Chemical characteristics

· **Workability:** Woods with high resin, oil or wax contents are difficult to work with. Petro accumulation and mineral salts originating from the soil that crystallize in the wood, also hinder workability.

· **Natural durability:** This is the resistance of the wood to attacks from destructive agents. This is important when the wood is to be found in conditions where there are changes to moisture that are superior to 18%. The agents can be fungi, xylophagous insects, (coleopterans and termites) and water xylophagous insects. Durability refers to the duramen (the alburnum is always vulnerable to attack) and is classified as durable, sensitive and non-durable.

· **Impregnability:** Resistance of wood to the penetration of liquid. Wood that is not durable but impregnable may be resistant against xylophagous attacks. Classification is as follows:
   Impregnable: Easy to impregnate with pressurized mechanisms.
   Average impregnability: Average penetration attained after 2 or 3 hours of treatment.
   Low impregnability: Only superficial impregnation achieved after 3 or 4 hours.
   Zero impregnability (or non-impregnability): Practically impossible to impregnate.

ABIES alba Mill. (ABETO) Silver fir

This is a readily available conifer of European origin.

Physical properties: It is of average density with a density of 400kg/m^3, soft (1.4), cuts easily, has little resin, is moisture resistant, and has straight grain.

Mechanical properties: It glues well but is a bit delicate for nailing and screwing. It finishes well but does not absorb finishings uniformly but rather manifests different intensities and colors.

Natural durability: It is not very durable as it is fungi and insect sensitive.

Impregnability: The duramen has low to average impregnability and the alburnum average.

Uses: Exterior, decorative veneers, furniture, and laminated wood.

ACER pseudoplatanus L. (ARCE) Sycamore

It is a readily available broadleaf from Europe and Asia.

Physical properties: It is of average density with a density of 610-680 kg/m^3, semi-hard (4.7) and very abrasion resistant. It has straight and wavy grain. It is good for steam shaping.

Mechanical properties: It glues, nails, and screws well. It finishes well.

Natural durability: It is not durable (fungi) and is sensitive to insects.

Impregnability: It is easily impregnable.

Uses: Interior carpentry (floors), decorative veneers, furniture, and cabinetmaking.

ANCOUMEA klaineana Pierre (OKUME)

It is a readily available broadleaf from Central Africa.

Physical properties: density with a density of 430-450 kg/m^3. It is soft (1.5) and has a straight or spiral grain.

Mechanical properties: It glues, nails, and screws well. Wood putty can be used for finishing it.

Natural durability: It is not very durable as it is affected by fungi and is sensitive to insects.

Impregnability: The duramen has low impregnability.

Uses: Plywood panels, interior carpentry with decorative veneering, furniture, and cabinetmaking.

BETULA alba L. (ABEDUL) Birch

It is a broadleaf from Europe that is quite readily available.

Physical properties: It is of average density with a density of 640-670 kg/m³, semi-hard (2.7-5.3) and has a straight grain. Its qualities make it an excellent choice for structural plywood.

Mechanical properties: It glues well. Drilling is required before nailing and screwing. It can be finished well.

Natural durability: It is not durable (fungi) and is sensitive to insects.

Impregnability: It affords easy to average impregnability.

Uses: Plywood panels, top-quality carpentry, decorative veneering, and furniture.

BETULA alleghaniensis Britt. (ABEDUL AMARILLO) Yellow birch

It is a broadleaf from Canada and The United States that is a bit scarce.

Physical properties: It is of average density with a density of 550-710 kg/m³, semi-hard (harder than birch). It has straight grain, it is easy to work, and has good resistance to bending, compression and blows.

Mechanical properties: It glues well. Drilling is required before nailing and screwing. It can be finished well.

Natural durability: It is not durable (fungi) and is sensitive to insects.

Impregnability: It affords easy to average impregnability.

Uses: Plywood panels, top-quality carpentry, decorative veneering, furniture, and floors.

CASTANEA sativa Mill. (CASTAÑO) Sweet chesnut

It is a broadleaf from Europe (from around the Mediterranean) that is quite readily available.

Physical properties: It is of slight density with a density of 540-650 kg/m³ and is soft (2.1). It has a slightly wavy grain. When moisture is present, it speeds up metal corrosion and turns blue.

Mechanical properties: It glues, nails, and screws well. Wood putty should be used for finishing it.

Natural durability: It is not very durable as it is fungi and insect sensitive.

Impregnability: The duramen is easily impregnable and the alburnum is of average impregnability.

Uses: Carpentry (doors, windows, and floors) and cabinetmaking.

CHAMAECYPARIS nootkatensis Spach. (CEDRO) Yellow Cedar

It is a broadleaf from North America that is quite readily available.

Physical properties: It is of slight density with a density of 430-530 kg/m^3 and is semi-hard. It has a straight grain and is acid-resistant.

Mechanical properties: It glues, nails, and screws well.

Natural durability: It is of average durability (fungi) and sensitivity (insects). It is durable against water xylophagous insects.

Impregnability: The duramen has low impregnability and the alburnum has good impregnability.

Uses: Interior and exterior carpentry, decorative veneering, furniture, and cabinetmaking.

CHLOROPHORA excelsa Benth (IROKO)

It is a broadleaf of African origin that is readily available.

Physical properties: It is of average density whose density is 630-650-670 kg/m^3. It is semi-hard and has straight grain.

Mechanical properties: It glues, nails, and screws well. Wood putty can be used for finishing it.

Natural durability: It is very durable against fungi, and durable against termites. It is easily attacked by water xylophagous insects.

Impregnability: The duramen has non-impregnability and the alburnum is easily impregnable.

Uses: Structural plywood panels, interior and exterior carpentry, decorative veneering, furniture, cabinetmaking, and laminated wood. It can be a substitute for teak.

ENTANDROPHRAGMA cylindricum Sprague. (SAPELLI) Sapele

It is a broadleaf of African origin that is quite readily available.

Physical properties: It is of average density with a density of 640-700 kg/m^3 and is semi-hard (3.6-4.2). It has a spiral grain. It can ooze resin and have a rough grainy surface.

Mechanical properties: It glues, nails, and screws well, and has a good finish.

Natural durability: It has average durability against fungi, is very durable against insects and is sensitive to water xylophagous insects.

Impregnability: The duramen has low impregnability and the alburnum has average impregnability.

Uses: Plywood, interior and exterior carpentry, decorative veneering, furniture, and cabinetmaking.

FAGUS sylvatica L. (HAYA) Common beech

This is a readily available broadleaf from Western Europe.

Physical properties: It is of average density with a density of 690-750 kg/m³, is semi-hard (4) and has straight grain.

Mechanical properties: It glues, nails, and screws well. Wood putty should be used for finishing it.

Natural durability: It is not durable against fungi and is sensitive to insects.

Impregnability: It is easily impregnable

Uses: Interior carpentry (floors), decorative veneering, furniture, cabinetmaking (especially for curved pieces)

FRAXINUS excelsior L. (FRESNO) Ash

It is readily available broadleaf of Northern African, Eastern Asian, and European origin.

Physical properties: It is of rather high density with a density of 680-750 kg/m³. It is semi-hard (4-5.3), has straight grain and good curve.

Mechanical properties: It glues well. Drilling is required before nailing and screwing. It can be finished well.

Natural durability: It is not durable against fungi and is sensitive to insects.

Impregnability: It is easily impregnable.

Uses: Decorative veneering and floors.

HYMENEA spp. (JATOBA)

It is a broadleaf from South America that is abundant but production of it is scarce.

Physical properties: It is of rather high density with a density of 955-970 kg/m³. It is hard (8), has straight grain and may have tension wood and pitch pockets.

Mechanical properties: It glues well (interiors). Drilling is required before nailing and screwing. It can be finished well.

Natural durability: It is durable in respect to fungi and insects but it is sensitive to water xylophagous insects.

Impregnability: The duramen has low impregnability.

Uses: Interior and exterior carpentry (floors, stairs), decorative veneering, furniture, and cabinetmaking.

INTSIA bijuga O. Ktze. L. (MERBAU)

It is broadleaf that comes from Southeast Asia and Oceania that is difficult to obtain.

Physical properties: It is of average density with a density of 730-830 kg/m³. It is hard (6.4), has straight or spiral grain and has an oily touch due to gum, silica and sulfur deposits. It stains if it comes in contact with metal.

Mechanical properties: It glues well and drilling is required before nailing and screwing. The surface must be duly prepared before finishing.

Natural durability: It is very durable against fungi and of average durability against insects.

Impregnability: Very good impregnability.

Uses: Exterior carpentry (windows) and interior (floors, stairs), decorative veneering, furniture, and cabinetmaking.

JUGLANS regia-nigra L. (NOGAL) Walnut tree

It is readily available broadleaf from North America, Europe, Asia, and Northern Africa.

Physical properties: It is of slight density with a density of 550-680 kg/m³. It is semi-hard (3.2-3.6) and has straight grain.

Mechanical properties: It glues, nails, and screws well and has a good finish.

Natural durability: It is of average durability against fungi and is sensitive to insects.

Impregnability: The duramen has low impregnability and the alburnum is very impregnable.

Uses: Interior carpentry (paneling, floors), decorative veneering, furniture, and cabinetmaking.

KHAYA ivorensis A. Chev. (CAOBA) Mahogany

It is readily available broadleaf of Western African origin.

Physical properties: It is of average density with a density of 490-530 kg/m³. It is soft (1.9) and has straight grain.

Mechanical properties: It glues, nails, and screws well and wood putty should be used before finishing it.

Natural durability: It is of average durability against fungi and is sensitive to insects.

Impregnability: The duramen is non-impregnable and the alburnum has average impregnability.

Uses: Plywood panels, interior and exterior carpentry, decorative veneering, furniture, and cabinetmaking. It can be a substitute for sapele.

LARIX dedicua Mill. (ALERCE) Larch

It is readily available conifer from Central Europe and North America.

Physical properties: It is of rather high density with a density of 470-650 kg/m3. It is semi-hard (2.2-3.2), has straight grain and wide vessels.

Mechanical properties: It glues well and nails and screws well if fine tips are used. It has a resinous finish.

Natural durability: It shows little durability against fungi and is sensitive to insects.

Impregnability: The duramen is practically impossible to impregnate and the alburnum is of average impregnability.

Uses: Plywood boards, paneling, interior carpentry (floors), and decorative veneering.

MILLETIA laurentil De Wild. (WENGÉ)

It is broadleaf of African origin with average availability.

Physical properties: It is of rather high density with a density of 700-900 kg/m3. It is hard (9), has straight grain, is durable and resinous.

Mechanical properties: It is a bit delicate to glue and drilling is required previous to nailing and screwing. The finishing must be done with wax-based products.

Natural durability: It is durable against fungi and insects do not attack it.

Impregnability: The duramen is non-impregnable.

Uses: Interior and exterior carpentry (floors), decorative veneering, furniture, and cabinetmaking.

OLEA europaea L. (OLIVO) Olive tree

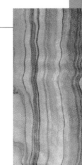

It is broadleaf that comes from the Mediterranean region, is of average availability but production is scarce.

Physical properties: It is of rather high density with a density of 850-1.120 kg/m3. It is hard, has an irregular grain and an oily touch.

Mechanical properties: Gluing is difficult due to its oiliness. Drilling is required before nailing and screwing. It finishes well.

Natural durability: Durable

Impregnability: The duramen has low impregnability and the alburnum is of easy impregnability.

Uses: Interior carpentry (floors), decorative veneering, and furniture.

PINUS radiata D. Don (PINO INSIGNIS) Radiata pine

It is a readily available conifer that comes from the southeast of Europe, New Zealand, and Australia.

Physical properties: It is of average density with a density of 500 kg/m³. It is semi-hard (1.8) and has straight grain.

Mechanical properties: It glues well (permeable) and nails and screws well too. Putty should be used before finishing.

Natural durability: It is not very durable against fungi and is sensitive to insects.

Impregnability: The duramen is practically impossible to impregnate and the alburnum is of average to low impregnability.

Uses: Structural plywood boards, exterior carpentry (laminated trimmings) and interior (paneling), laminated wood, and furniture.

PINUS sylvestris L. (PINO SILVESTRE) Redwood

It is readily available conifer that comes from the north of Asia and Europe.

Physical properties: It is of slight density with a density of 500-540 kg/m³. It is semi-hard (2), has straight grain and resinous vessels.

Mechanical properties: The resinous characteristic of it must be taken into account when gluing. It nails and screws well. To finish it well, it must be thoroughly dried.

Natural durability: It is little durable against fungi and sensitive to insects.

Impregnability: The duramen has zero impregnability but the alburnum is easily impregnable.

Uses: Plywood boards, interior and exterior carpentry (doors, paneling, floors), decorative veneering, furniture, cabinetmaking, and laminated wood.

POPULUS alba L. (CHOPO) Poplar

It is a readily available broadleaf that comes from Europe, Asia, and Northern Africa.

Physical properties: It is of average density with a density of 420-480 kg/m³. It is soft (1.2-2.6) and has straight grain.

Mechanical properties: It glues well but nailing and screwing are average. The finishing must be done against the grain.

Natural durability: It is little durable against fungi and sensitive to insects.

Impregnability: The duramen has low impregnability but the alburnum is easily impregnable.

Uses: Plywood boards.

PSEUDOTSUGA menziessii Franco (PINO OREGON) Douglas fir

It is a readily available conifer that comes from North America, the United Kingdom, and Australia.

Physical properties: It is of average density with a density of 470-520 kg/m3. It is semi-hard (2.2) and has straight grain.

Mechanical properties: It glues well, though it may undergo coloration, and it nails and screws well. The finishing requires preparation.

Natural durability: It is of average durability and is sensitive to insects.

Impregnability: The duramen is non-impregnable and the alburnum is of average or low impregnability.

Uses: Plywood, floors, and interior or exterior carpentry.

QUERCUS robur L. (ROBLE) Oak

It is readily-available broadleaf from Europe, Asia Minor, and Northern Africa.

Physical properties: It is of average density with a density of 670-760 kg/m3. It is semi-hard (3.5-4.4) and has straight grain. It can corrode metal. It can be easily bent with steam.

Mechanical properties: It glues well and drilling is required before nailing and screwing. Putty should be used for the finishing.

Natural durability: It is durable against fungi but sensitive to insects.

Impregnability: The duramen is non-impregnable but the alburnum is easily impregnable.

Uses: Interior carpentry (floors), decorative veneering, furniture, and cabinetmaking.

QUERCUS rubra L. (ROBLE ROJO) Red oak

It is a readily available broadleaf of North American origin.

Physical properties: It is of average density with a density of 650-790 kg/m3. It is semi-hard (3.5-4.5) and has straight grain. It discolors on contact with metal and moisture and bends easily with steam.

Mechanical properties: Care must be taken with gluing as some glues work better than others. Drilling is required before nailing and screwing and putty should be used for the finishing.

Natural durability: It is little durable against fungi and sensitive to insects.

Impregnability: The duramen has low to average impregnability and the alburnum is easily impregnable.

Uses: Plywood boards, interior carpentry (floors), decorative veneering, furniture, and cabinetmaking.

Directory

ACKNOWLEDGEMENTS:

We wish to thank all of the people who have collaborated (at times, far beyond the call of duty) in finding and sending us published material: proprietors, architects, designers, photographers, and office staff in architectural offices. Above all we would like to give special thanks to Daniel Nassar, a colleague and friend, and an expert on wood.